Cosy Sheridan's
partner

XMAS 2011

From
WOODY/EL

Works On Paper

WORKS ON PAPER

Poems & Illustrations By

TR RITCHIE

Whitebark Press
Moab

ISBN: 978-0-615-48049-7

Privately published by Whitebark Press; Moab UT
Printed in the United States of America

First Printing - March 2011
Second Printing - April 2011
Third Printing - July 2011
Fourth Printing – October 2011

Additional copies available: $11.95 each, plus $2.50 postage & shipping
(Slightly more internationally; please write for specifics) from:

TR Ritchie
PO Box 479
Moab, UT 84532
trrinutah@gmail.com
www.TRRitchie.com

In Memoriam
Michael Terry
1945 - 2011

one day we will reminisce
about the old days
and one of us will remark
remember how michael
was always there for us

and then one day
something will happen
and later in speaking of it
one of us will say
that happened
after michael

and in each case
michael will be with us

CONTENTS

FORWARD

TR Ritchie is an award-winning songwriter and a seasoned performer; he can charm the socks off a crowd when he's in the mood. He can also write poetry that flows like a wild river.

From his time as a fire lookout on Mule Peak in eastern Oregon to his days singing in Pike Street Market in Seattle to the present, TR has always had a notebook of some kind with him. The sketches and poems contained here span thirty years of his thoughtful, observant life - from 1979 to 2011.

I first heard TR's writing in song form at the Kerrville Folk Festival in Texas in 1992. I heard the phrase "sometimes small and twisted things can split the hardest stone" and I knew I had heard something beautiful and unusual. He has always been first and foremost a wordsmith; his songs are carefully crafted. Here in these poems he is like a strong bird flying free from restraint – and you can feel the energy moving through his words.

Everywhere we have gone together for the past 18 years, TR has brought his sketchbook. I am especially fond of his trees. His sketches are like he is: wild and very determined and yet open to being unsure of things.

We live in a desert landscape. It is distinct and sharply defined. TR's poems are like one green cottonwood tree in the mouth of the canyon, up against the redrock under blue sky, pointing towards the essential: showing us where the water is, where life is.

Cosy Sheridan
Moab 2011

ABOUT THE DRAWINGS

I began sketching during my summers as a fire lookout for the US Forest Service back in the late seventies. It was a perfect setting for it – things to draw at every turn and many idle hours. That first summer I worked in pencil, on sheets of typing paper, but since then I've always sketched in ink, straight to sketchbook without any preliminary outlining.

I work this way for two reasons: one, it requires that I take time to really examine a subject before I make my first move; and two, it's a continuing lesson in accepting whatever happens. Sometimes proportions go haywire and perspective gets skewed, but to me that's not necessarily a bad thing. The sketches were never meant to be photographic in their detail. Instead, they're a sort of journal without words which illustrates my life. Looking at them I'm not confined to a single narrative of those times and places. The story keeps changing. I like it that way. I think certain stories are better told *without* words.

ABOUT THE POEMS

Most of the poems in this book are recent, written in the last year or so, but two or three go way back, and I've included the lyrics to a couple of my songs, too, just because they seem to belong here. In my other life I'm a songwriter and musician. This time I'll leave it to you to find your own music in the quiet of these pages.

TR Ritchie

Works On Paper

What Is Still Wild Within Me

what is still wild within me
runs tonight beneath a waxing moon
yellow eyes laughing in defiance
of all things walled away
from wildness

to be alive to the bone
to the blood and fire
of raw existence
is this where we went wrong
to trade such wildness
for one long soft slide
toward sleep

Beauty Is There
Offering Itself

beauty is there offering itself
every day asking nothing
not even that you notice
the way light shines
through dry grass at sundown
or the way shadows lay themselves across
some arrangement of sandstone boulders
or how the crisp air moves in and out
as you climb an upward trail
blue mountains to the east
falling toward nightfall
taking you with them
and the sky opening its hands
to show you this star
then this one then these
yours for the taking
take them take all you want
the pockets of beauty
are bottomless

I Was Lucky When Young

i was lucky when young
to have life blow open
and show me
what was waiting
and to offer a choice
what is known
what is unknown
and having chosen
the gates swung closed
and all that remained
was to climb upon fortune's
heaving shoulders
twist my fist into its flying mane
hold on for dear life and ride

i am no horseman
but i have covered some ground

How Could Any Day
Fail To Be Worthy Of
The Poet's Eye

how could any day
fail to be worthy
of the poet's eye
an afternoon walk
beside the ice-rimmed creek
solitary ravens high in the
winter cottonwoods
yes every day they can be
counted upon for inspiration
yes every day the
glittering evidence
throws itself in my face
as if to ask which part
of these instructions
do you not understand

Stand Where You Are

stand where you are
just stand there
let the light fall upon your face
and across your shoulders
onto your arms and hands
onto your feet bare on the stone
feel how it celebrates your skin
how it rejoices that you are there
that it may in its way sing your name
haven't you always been deserving
of such praise
has it ever been easier
to be loved

Pretty Simple Really

pretty simple really
return to the wilds
or die
you think i'm kidding
i'm not
is proof what you want
absolute proof
irrefutable evidence
look around you
does this look like paradise

how though
one way only
you must give the wilds
your undivided
attention
you must abandon
the comfort of
your complacency
you must be willing
to be alone

Resolve To Listen

resolve to listen
to the voice within
that speaks to you
in quiet tones
like wind in the grass
like rain on the pines
like the sound
of the wild
creatures
breathing
that says to you
isn't it time...
what if...
is it possible...

move toward
the thing you were
born to do

as for the voices
who nag or scream
or threaten or shame
know them for the
liars they are
show compassion
for their desperate ways
forgive them
turn away

move then
toward the thing
you were born to do

Blessed By Hindsight

blessed by hindsight
i offer thanks
to whatever gods may be
that my prayers have not
been answered
not one
i ask you now
what kind of luck is that

Forget Everything

forget everything
that is to say
lay aside your
troubles for a moment
dwell not on regrets
time out from your dreams
turn the clock
to the wall
turn off
your cell phones
shut down your
computer
now
step outside
close your eyes
stand there
listen to the world
a miracle
is it not
that we're all
still together here

If Necessary I Will Steal You
From The Life That Wants
To Cage You

if necessary i will
steal you from the life
that wants to cage you
i will return you to
the wilds don't
think i won't
we will do what we
have to do in the
name of wildness

we will be
outlaws together
laughing across a
rough-hewn table
in some remote
canyon cabin
running our hands
up and through the golden
bounty of our stolen
moments hours days years
letting each tumble back
in a chaotic racket of
clattering joy

Note To Self

close the notebook
put down the pen
words are like trout and you
have spooked them somehow
now they hover in the deeps
suspicious of your motives

sometimes you have to
rest the pool
now might be that time
leave your desk
go for a walk among the
waking trees of spring
look at the smiling face
of the meadow
put your hands in your pockets
and be satisfied
you'll have your poem
another day

Where Is Home They Ask

where is home they ask
and i tell them
down in the red rock country
and before that
the hills of seattle
and before that
the fields of oklahoma
and before that
the empty kansas plains

and before that
a country i'm on my way to
now over those hills
out there that way

i'll know that ground
when i get there

Empty Your Pockets And Climb

empty your pockets and climb
bring water a little food
a blanket because the nights can be chill
among the white boulders at the summit
we will build a fire and watch the stars rise
over the shoulder of the world
then stare the coals to ashes and sleep
in the morning you will be healed
i've seen it happen before
come
think nothing of it
your money's no good here

Trail Smarts

down
top
the
from
mountain
the
climb
cannot
work - you
of
line
this
in
you're
when
learn
soon
you
thing
one

MULE PEAK
DRAWINGS

Mule Peak Lookout, Eagle Cap Wilderness Area, Oregon

From 1978 to 1981 I was a forest service lookout in northeastern
Oregon, stationed two of those seasons at Mule Peak, a wilderness
lookout built in 1924 on what was then the Wallowa National
Forest. It was a steep four-mile walk up from the trailhead and at a
bit over 8500 feet was highest lookout on the forest. Some people
are bred-in the-blood lookouts and I am one of them. These drawings
are from that time in my life.

In Two Days Time The
World Dissolves

in two days time the banged and clattered
world dissolves to muted woods where fog
moves on the darkened dripping slopes and
jockeyed taxis of those mad contrived pursuits
cross-fade to big-eared deer that spook to
tangled thickets pause just out of sight stare back
to watch me shuffle through their chosen haunts

gone the rumbling streets
where scavengers of commerce prowl
and billboards grin their frozen perfect cures
to hungers of an unreal need
here a scuff through fallen cones and gathered duff
up solitary trails in boots well oiled to shed
the drizzled rain gladly barters labor for the gain
and shoulders cramped by recent narrow mobs
sag in plain relief with not the burdened
complications of a world but just this
loaded rucksack to be borne
after all the crazed racket down below
this silence turns a madman sane
squirrels barking down the misted lodgepole trunks
make a bigger sense than all the wireman's words

up a track that's known but paw and cloven hoof
the months between these lugsoled fits
my step is lighter by the hour
compared to climbing walls through intervals
of waited days it's blessed plight to face
so unambiguous a thing as just this
hump of mountain looming in my way

Mule Peak Lookout, looking southeast. Unlike most lookout stations, Mule Peak was aligned to the terrain of the ridgetop, not the compass. From this perspective the ridge falls away steeply to the left and right, and to the left lies the Eagle Cap Wilderness Area.

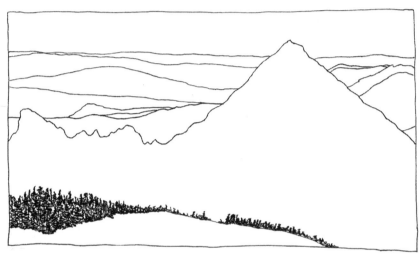

Burger Butte

Another one of Burger Butte. I loved the symmetry of this peak.

Whitebark Pine. These tough little trees anchor themselves in cracks in the granite and basalt outcrops of the peaks, where terrain and weather and time make them beautiful.

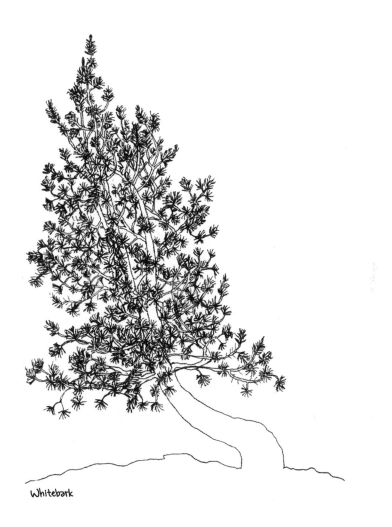

Whitebark

View into the head of South Catherine Creek from lookout doorway.

Flagstaff Butte. In the days before good roads there was once a lookout tower down there on the point.

Interior view, southeast corner. Scan this two-page spread clockwise for a sense of how the lookout was laid out.

Interior view northeast corner

Interior view, southwest corner

Interior view, northwest wall

Bad Company

they came noisy up the trail
the way their kind always do
stopped down the ridge
to tumble boulders from the heights
and cheer the frenzied destruction
of gravity and stone

flopped in my catwalk shade
consumed their packaged
lunchfoods
tipped canteens and
looked around as if they'd
seen it all before
agreed they'd go nuts sure
to live alone like me through
all these summer days

gone i got my broom
and swept their
footprints off my path
then pissed the grass
where they had sat
half an hour later heard them
off toward burger butte
shouting down the cliffs as if
they thought they had words
these high-blown slopes
had waited through a million
years to hear

The Osborne Firefinder, ubiquitous in lookouts since 1915. Invented by Portland forester William Osborne; originally manufactured by Leupold + Stevens, Inc. in Beaverton, Oregon.

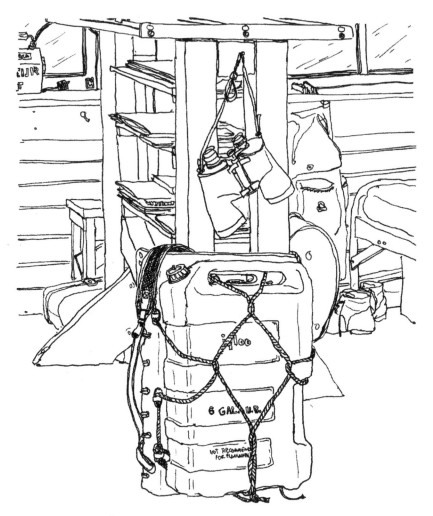

My water pack. Hardly ever used — snowbanks kept me well supplied for most of the season.

Boots and split wood

Night interior. Due to the lookout's elevation and the steepness of the ridge, the firefinder at Mule Peak was offset from center to allow for taking azimuths over the windowsill into the drainages below.

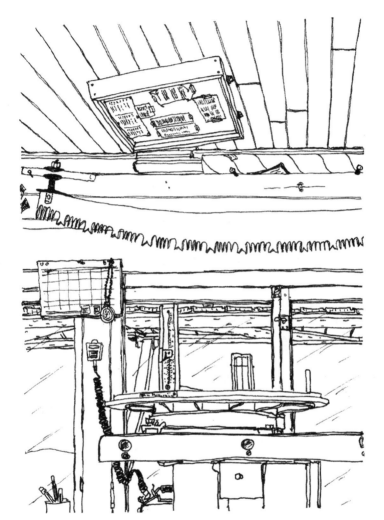

More interior details – firefinder, crosscut saw, ceiling swing-board.

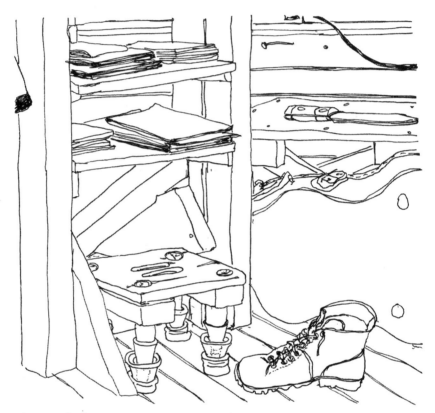

Lightning stool and boot. Lookout operators stand on these little stools for protection from lightning strikes during thunderstorms. I was lucky; Mule Peak never took a hit while I was there.

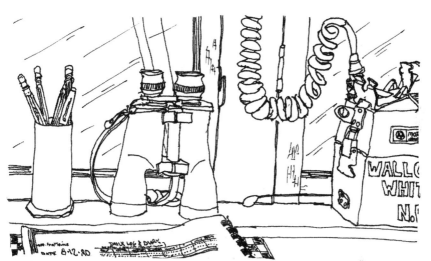

All business: radio daily logbook, 7 x 50s, Motorola radiophone.

Stove corner with pots and pans.

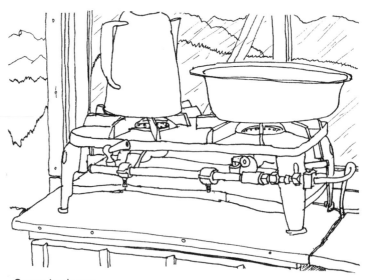

Propane two-burner

At Dusk The Conies

at dusk the conies creep
to outposts in the tumbled scree
and pause their tiny shapes
against the massive thrust
of buckled granite crust
throat their cries across the heights
and wait the coming of the night
past eagle cap
out of the hour the stars
begin to breathe
the wind goes off the slope
and twenty miles downriver
a lantern on the widow's walk
above the cliffs of prominence
blinks its yellow eye
and stares into the dark
the moon breaks past the rim of sky
and one by one the conies turn
to make their way to nests
beneath the rocks
now nothing moves
except a hand by candle light
trailing words across
the yielding page

Whitebark

this is the life I have been given
these are the seasons of my time
and I am seeking out the light
according to design
i've weathered storms I cannot count
to make this world my home
in a place where small and twisted things
can split the hardest stone

in one like me you might not see
how I have managed to exist
a fragile crooked rack of limbs
in terrain as rough as this
but to those who take their chances here
experience has shown
that sometimes small and twisted things
can split the hardest stone

so shed no tears of pity here
spin no tales of tragic grace

just let it be enough
that life is blooming in this rocky place
it is the proof that seeds will grow
wherever they are sown
and that sometimes small and twisted things
can split the hardest stone

Once For A Hundred Days

once for a hundred days
i walked the same way
through a mountain meadow
twice a month to town and back
making a path where none had been

thirty years passed and i returned
to find the same path
faint but unmistakable
still reminding the world
i had come that way

do not think
your slightest gesture
goes unnoticed

Maybe Things Get Worse

maybe things get worse
maybe everything is torn apart
then maybe the world gets quiet
and the ones who remain
will have another try at eden
plant apple orchards
become snake handlers
call things by their real names
maybe this time we'll get it right

One Too Many Sodden Days

one too many sodden days
above elliott bay could be
to blame for this
or the ghost of who I
once was still living
restless for misremembered things
anyway the etchings of barren trees
scratched into this somber sky
leaves me a stranger even
among faces i recognize
and the coffee
salvation for melancholy moods
on days like this
not as good by half

Rendered

rendered
speechless
by one
stunned
moment
of recognition
i have
spent years
searching for
words to match
the taste
of such
sweet defeat

Contours

into the rough surface
of experience i carve
the contours of one
flawless moment

the thought of you
is like a tool
perfectly weighted
and balanced
to fit my hand

The Cooper's Hawk

the cooper's hawk has taken a
band-tailed pigeon and now feathers
drift across the snow and lodge
against the dry grasses by the fence
i open my door and step into the winter sun
kneel and lift a blood-flecked feather
shade my eyes and look to the western cliffs

already the sparrows are emerging from
the tangled row of rose bushes

How Serenely She Rests

how serenely she rests
at the center of her creation
motionless as the remains
of distant ancestors
preserved in amber
across this arc of
twenty-six million years
for them for her
the same covenant
the universe teems
with sustenance
all one need do
is spread one's web
and wait

Sparrows Again

sparrows again
ganged in the leafless
brush of the fencerow
shouting their gratitudes
to the world
so commonplace a sight
as to go unnoticed
but have you looked lately
into the black fire
of their wild eyes
can you say your own life
crackles with such passion
for the moment

have you ever dared
to bear the weight of
such surrender
what courage would it take
to live like sparrows

Now Then Snow

now then snow
falling briefly on the golden hearts
of cottonwood leaves
and on the mountains
clouds like i recall
of darkened northwest afternoons
rainslick seattle streets alive with lights
and the mutter of rain against windowpanes
where encamped in solitary rooms
i summoned music from thin air

it is possible then
to be two places at once
here and also there among
remnants of a season
one half flesh and blood
striking at these keys
the other a ghostly time traveler
drifting like mist past
yellow windows in the dusk

listen
a note far off
like a bell-buoy in the harbor
rocking on the tide
to mark the edge of safety
and beckon home all who walk
the edges of the world

And Isn't It A Grace

and isn't it a grace
that on the longest night of the year
the moon should shine so bright as this
offering itself as compensation
for the way things need be arranged
to keep a universe in order

If It Were Easy

sometimes
the best
and only hope
is to gut it out
endure
stumble up
from the ashes
of your phoenix
and begin again
the ungraceful work
of learning to fly

do you think you
have a choice
if it were easy
anyone could do it

We Were All Gods

we were all gods
we could disappear here
and reappear
a thousand miles away
we could transform anything
into money
love hunger work
leisure suffering death
we could see what wasn't there
and hear what we wanted
we had the power
to grant wishes
to punish without mercy
the spooks we worshiped
looked exactly like us
we bowed our heads
and all was forgiven
it was our world
a garden of eden
the promised land
paradise on earth
oh we had it good
we did we did
we were all gods
we were
it was the golden age
of predators

See How The Sun

see how the sun
lights the red walls
well past five these
cold afternoons

beneath the
frozen ground
of the garden
tulip bulbs
tick away
like time bombs

I Am Encouraged By The Buds

i am encouraged by the buds
that offer me their promise
here in this winter sun
and the pale wash of willow green
against a january sky
drawing my eye upward
away from the snowbound earth
toward distant horizons
as if any reminder is needed
even on the coldest day
renewal smolders

My People Tired

my people tired of
rocky appalachian hollows
wandered on west
to empty plains
where i discontent
with emptiness
went further
until the ground
reached up
and claimed me

unjealous
it let me trek
its width and breadth
for trekking too
is home together
ground and motion
make history
mine spelled out
in worn-down boots
flung to the tops
of cottonwoods
along backroad blacktops

little by little
the wind will have its way
and you should look to find me
if you ever have that need
snagged by cactus thorn
or sagebrush
scattered all the way from
where i ever was
to where i ever
longed to be

SEATTLE
DRAWINGS

3825 Whitman Avenue North; Seattle

Seattle was my home for seventeen years. I moved there in 1973 and began my
musical life singing for tips on the street at the Pike Street Market and in
the little cafes of Fremont and Pioneer Square. My last apartment was a
studio in the back of this house just off the north end of the Aurora Bridge
on old highway 99. In 1991 it was razed to make way for another apartment
building, but by then I was already on the road a lot, heading for a bigger
world. I wrote some good songs there. These are a few of my drawings from
that time in my life.

My place in the back, door on the right - Unit 5. Rent was $200 a month, never raised the 6 years I lived there - utilities included. A sweet deal.

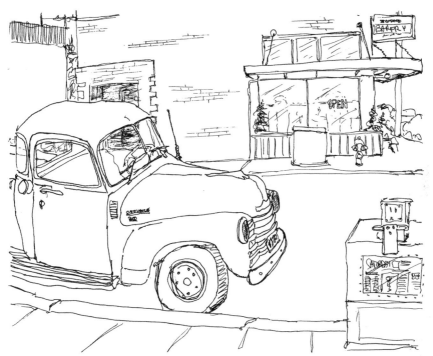

Scene from a coffeehouse window — '51 Chevy pick-up on Queen Ann Hill; Seattle sometime in the 80's.

Swingside Cafe Guest Check; Fremont Avenue; Seattle — four blocks from my house and one of my frequent haunts.

Lake Union Work Boats; Seattle - a mile down the hill from my place.

The MV Spokane making the Bainbridge Island / Seattle run. When I first moved to Seattle I lived on the island for a while and made this crossing a lot. The ferry docked at the foot of Marion Street, a short walk down to Pioneer Square and up to the Pike Street Market.

Discovery Park Lighthouse; Seattle

Fremont Bridge; Seattle

Triangle building; 1st Avenue South; Seattle – I had a part-time job on the third floor of a building across the street for a couple of years.

The Antique Sandwich Company; Tacoma. Home of the long-running Victory Music open mic, still going strong after all these years. Epicenter of the Puget Sound acoustic music community then and now.

I Wait Here At The Edge Of Silence

i wait here at the edge of silence
the smooth page spread before me
like an open meadow rising
to a line of trees and a dark forest

it's getting late
but that doesn't bother me
evening is often the best time
and i am good at waiting
once i sat so still
a junco flew from the thickets
and alighted on my knee
its small feet through the
canvas of my pant leg feeling like
a tiny set of keys capable of unlocking
the mysteries of the world

sometimes the wait yields nothing
the light is going fast
i resign myself to hunger
hunger being the hunter's own muse
then something moves
up the hill there yes
my eyes widen
the moment arrives
like deer drifting down
from the shelter of the trees
one by one
words begin to come

Some Of These Side Canyons
Go Nowhere

some of these side canyons go nowhere
nothing back there but tangled oak poison ivy
maybe an old cottonwood in the sand
below some slickrock pour-off
certainly no trail nothing on the map
nothing to recommend it
you'll see lizards beetles maybe a raven
one thing though it'll be quiet
still enough to hear the
one-note dirge of the world
where you come from
have you known such things
no then
maybe you've arrived
maybe what you need is such terrain
to flush the noise and brainrot
from your life
you're in luck
this time of day
the snakes are in their dens

North Of Klamath Falls

north of klamath falls
ninety-seven turns to ice
and suddenly the road
gets interesting
in the same way
the woods look different
when you realize
the day's getting dark
clouds have gathered and
you have lost the trail
now the journey
becomes a meditation
upon a single question
and the answer a heckling
remorseless tease
maybe you will
and
maybe
you won't

Doe

passing her
sad mangled
carcass
splayed by
the roadside
i don't suppose
the loss of
this one doe
will make much
difference
to the world
but
what if it did

Contained

contained
by space
tamed by
patience
the wild
beast
purrs

All Day Discontent

all day discontent has been
crashing around inside me
like a bird trapped in a room
i have opened every window
but it refuses to leave
throwing itself instead
at the ceiling and high corners
convinced in its panic
that there is no way out
look look i plead look
the windows are open
release is there right there
but it continues to flail
bruising its wings and breastbone
pushing us both toward exhaustion
let night come quickly then
maybe darkness is the answer
perhaps by morning
i will awaken
in a quiet place

Today The Cherry Tree

today the cherry tree
opened its first
white palm to the sun
this
could be mistaken
for a beginning

and today a friend
sits in shadow
waiting for death
this
could be mistaken
for an ending

and today i want to believe
there is more to both of these
than what they seem
that there is sorrow
somewhere in blossoms
and beauty somewhere in death
but this
could be mistaken
for understanding

My Old Enemy Waits

my old enemy waits patiently
all it takes is one mistake
one careless moment
and there it is
the double-guess of
uncertainty
the beautiful lies
of reason
and i
defenseless
in the face of those
must accept the blows
be staggered
take the hard fall
then find it in myself
to rise
shake it off
offer a blood-lipped grin
and ask
so is that all you got

Houses Half Buried

houses half buried
in this railroad town
and snow still falling
on the big river's dark water
twelve hundred miles
above astoria
dig out drive west
today i'm suffering to recall
when i last read jack london
but the dogs are fed and healthy
and my hands are warm

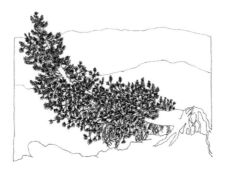

Refuge Among Produce
On A Cold Day

these cold winter days
i warm my hands
over the glowing coals of oranges
and bask in harvest sunlight
stored in the firm curved bodies
of peppers and pears

melons from mexico
invite me to lie down
among them
to know better
the hot dry ground

bananas motion southward
with their curved fingers
down where they come from
grown men have
never seen snow

surrounded by regiments
of summer color
i prolong my search
for the perfect apple
impatience
the master warns
will only leave me
discontent

In A Stove In A Room
In A House In A Town

In a stove
in a room
in a house
in a town
in a move of
overdue surrender
i commit to softwood flame
letters of an old affair
and watch them
curl and disappear
leaving me to
my unplanned delight
one final lovely gift
of heat
and light

Five Haikus

in the fog are pines
the sun burns the fog away
not a needle stirs

+++

the raven's shadow
slides across the canyon wall
gone without a trace

+++

the old juniper
beaten and battered by time
still waves one green flag

+++

ice in the potholes
where the sun does not yet shine
but look a lizard

+++

rain drums on tentflaps
snug here in my sleeping bag
i read all morning

+++

Back To Mountains

back to mountains
i am home again
writing my signature
with bootprints
on the forest floor
beside dark flanks
of douglas fir
once my dreams were
filled with mountain trails
leading up always up
to windy places
where snow survived
among the shadows into summer
up there the view was grand
i could see a long way
any which way i looked
and inward
even further

Rites

so it turns out
the simplest things
are the holiest

ask any dying friend

morning coffee
evening walks
laughter
work of the hands
shared meals
every day we engage
in sacrament without
fanfare or ceremony
and in the end it is not
extraordinary achievement
we find ourselves craving
but humble rites
which keep us
close to the ground
close to the moment
close to each other

let us honor the dying
by our earnest and
abiding allegiance
to ordinary grace

Here Is A Letter

here is a letter to you
begun on dark highways
wet in the iowa rain
carried to bright lighted chain restaurants
at crossroads in places with names i need not know
here is a letter walking your way
carried by a heart and a hand
and a hope: it is what we say
when we have nothing to say that counts
it is what we do when we
have nothing to do that reveals
the nature of our choices

to the west the cranes are sleeping
hugging the ground like shallow fog
except they are living fog

do they dream

do they remember last year's grainfields
last year's northern marshes
in their sleeps are they fledglings crying for food
how do they know what they know
as surely as these ten thousand cranes
i too am migrating
drawn by something i cannot name
something awakens and says: this way. come.
you are like the field where i was born
in my sleeps i would know you
in the dark in the twisting clouds that churn
across the face of continents

the night man sweeps
midnight like a white line on the highway
flashes past my headlamps

the cook a lanky kid with ears that stick out
slaps yet another burger on the grill
shoves a gravied meal at sleepy waitresses
chimes: one to go

I'm one
I go

the land goes down
the sky goes down
the land rises likewise the sky
always they touch
like new lovers unwilling to part
look at this: four billion years together
and still inseparable
even in these modern times
the answer is always there
love is just a matter of learning how to see
nor must this be rushed
these dark miles of rain
these toll booths and restless rest stops
these pods of diesel freighters
parked head to tail rumbling motionless
while their drivers sleep
even in this i tell myself be wakeful
it is passing do not miss it
never again will i cross to you
for the first time there's only once
and once should not be rushed
too much light too much tiled floor
too little sleep and endlessly it seems:
the highway

here's another day
eternity turned to a fresh page
and this moment the point of my pen

last night I'm wondering how big the soul
without the body would I know

a whale from a cricket
is god all the same spark
where is the edge of a sparrow
is my own soul carried kangaroo fashion
in an unseen pouch larger or smaller
than this vessel of bones
or is the body something like a lens
focusing sunlight into a hot white dot

god leapt onto the pavement
in the shape of a rabbit
i swerved
that was a close one

somehow the snow falling through this
spring afternoon is perfect
i would have written clear weather
and improbable warmth
i come from places
where april means go barefoot
sit on the front steps with guitars
listen to children playing on the sidewalk
watch the trees burst slowly to leaf
but after all this rain
what better surprise than snow
up over these hardwood mountains
down to New England saltwater on the strange side
where you're doing laundry as I roll up ninety-five
back forth round and round
motion will serve desire
and everything comes out
clean and sparkling in the end

metaphors are everywhere

Quiet Hands

after all is said and done
after my time has come and gone
let my life have been the scene
of useful work and graceful things
and i will rest with quiet hands
i will rest with quiet hands

DRAWINGS
FROM THE FIELD

Backyard view; boyhood home in Oklahoma. The street out front is Main Street

Chickaskia River; Blackwell, Oklahoma

Diversion dam on Chikaskia River, Northern Oklahoma

Dirt road. Northern Oklahoma

Long Pond; Omega Institute; Rhinebeck NY – I spent a month each summer for a few years as artist-in-residence at Omega.

Cafe at Omega Institute; Rhinebeck NY

Black Canyon of the Gunnison; Colorado

Falls of the Yellowstone; Wyoming

West side of the Elkhorn Ridge above Sumpter, Oregon

Stillwater River country, Montana

Crested Butte, Colorado

Two buildings, Crested Butte, Colorado

Starvation Peak, New Mexico

Somewhere above Paonia, Colorado

Mendocino, California

Big Sur, above Soberanes Creek

Niagara Falls, NY

Birch trees, somewhere up the Hudson River.

Colorado River; upstream from Moab

Colorado River; looking downstream from Portal

Backside of Main Street, Moab. I love alleys – they show how we really live.

Portal view from Moab

Cable Arch above Kane Creek: Moab

Juniper above Moonflower Canyon; Moab

Juniper above Cable Arch, Moab

ABOUT THE AUTHOR

TR Ritchie is a songwriter and touring musician, part-time graphic artist, photographer, tinker and thinker...as well as artist and poet. He lives in Moab, Utah with his partner Cosy Sheridan and 2 and 3/4 cats. *Works On Paper* is his first book.

ORIGINAL MUSIC BY TR RITCHIE

Wild Horses - released 2010

My Father's Wildest Dream – released 2003

Homeground – released 1995

Changing Of The Guard – released 1990

Not Just Another Pretty Songwriter – released 1985

All titles available at TR Ritchie's website:

www.TRRitchie.com

Or by mail.
$15 each, plus $1.50 postage.
(more for international postage)

TR Ritchie
PO Box 479
Moab, Utah 84532
USA

If you enjoyed this book, please recommend it to a friend.

Thanks.

TR.Rithhie